HOW TO DRAW Cute Animals

by Kathryn Clay

illustrated by June Brigman

Capstone press®

Mankato, Minnesota

Snap Books are published by Capstone Press,
151 Good Counsel Drive, P.O. Box 669, Mankato, Minnesota 56002.
www.capstonepress.com

Books published by Capstone Press are manufactured with paper
containing at least 10 percent post-consumer waste.

Library of Congress Cataloging-in-Publication Data
Clay, Kathryn.
    How to draw cute animals / by Kathryn Clay; illustrated by June Brigman.
    p. cm. — (Snap books. Drawing fun)
    Includes bibliographical references and index.
    Summary: "Lively text and fun illustrations describe how to draw cute animals" — Provided by publisher.
    ISBN: 978-1-4296-3405-2 (library binding)
    1. Animals in art — Juvenile literature. 2. Drawing — Technique — Juvenile literature. I. Brigman, June.
II. Title. III. Series.
NC780.C58 2010
743.6 — dc22
                                                 2009005788

Credits
Juliette Peters, designer
Abbey Fitzgerald, colorist

Photo Credits
Capstone Press/TJ Thoraldson Digital Photography, 4 (pencil), 5 (all), 32 (pencil)

The author dedicates this book to Emerson and Sebastian.

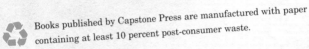

Table of Contents

Getting Started

Cute animals come in all shapes and sizes. They can be fat, furry, short, or spotty. With so much variety, it's no wonder that many artists enjoy drawing animals. Test your artistic skills by drawing these cute animals.

Are you fascinated by felines? Try sketching the napping kitten. Maybe you find Australian animals irresistible? Then practice drawing the kangaroo and koala. If you think cute animals don't always come covered in fur, then check out the red-eyed tree frog.

Of course, there are all kinds of cute animals. Maybe you think there's nothing more charming than a cow. Or perhaps you're fond of ferrets. Once you've mastered the basics in this book, you'll be able to draw pods, packs, herds, and flocks of cute animals.

Must-Have Materials

1. First you'll need something to draw on. Any blank, white paper will work well.

2. Pencils are a must for these drawing projects. Be sure to keep a bunch nearby.

3. Because sharp pencils make clean lines, you'll be sharpening those pencils a lot. Have a pencil sharpener handy.

4. Even the best artist needs to erase a line now and then. Pencil erasers wear out fast. A rubber or kneaded eraser will last much longer.

5. To make your drawings pop off the page, use colored pencils or markers.

Rabbit

Rabbits have tails that look like cotton balls and ears that stick up like antennas. They also have soft, shiny fur. With features like these, rabbits are easy to love. That is, unless you're a carrot farmer.

Try drawing a lop-eared rabbit with floppy ears.

STEP 1

STEP 2

STEP 3

STEP 4

Duckling

Have you ever tried walking with flippers on your feet? That's what ducks do every time they leave the water. While great for swimming, webbed feet make it difficult for ducks to walk on land. That's why they're always waddling.

Once you've mastered one duckling, draw several ducklings swimming in a pond.

STEP 1

STEP 2

STEP 3

STEP 4

Kangaroo and Joey

Kangaroos have long, flat feet. Their strong legs allow them to leap across the Australian outback. A kangaroo baby, called a joey, goes along for the ride tucked safely in the mother's pouch.

Draw this kangaroo jumping in midair.

STEP 1

STEP 2

STEP 3

STEP 4

Kitten

Kittens are fun to draw because they always end up in interesting places. Sometimes they're sitting on a windowsill. Other times they're sneaking into a sock drawer. This young feline chose someone's shoe as the perfect place for a catnap.

When kittens aren't sleeping, they're playing. Draw this kitten chasing a toy mouse.

STEP 1

STEP 2

STEP 3

STEP 4

Koala

Get close enough to a koala and you might smell something odd. That's because koalas live in eucalyptus trees and eat more than 1,000 leaves each day. The strong scent is absorbed into their thick, wooly fur.

Draw this koala eating a handful of eucalyptus leaves.

STEP 1

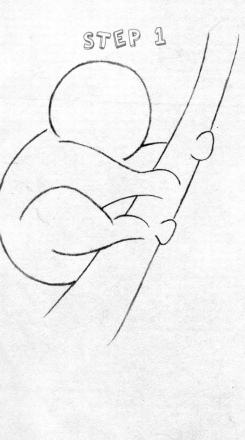

STEP 2

STEP 3

STEP 4

15

Meerkat

This long, lean member of the mongoose family stands straight up when it senses danger. Meerkats live in the wild grasslands and deserts of southern Africa. They're always on the lookout for fierce animals that roam the savanna.

Try drawing a meerkat clan. Grab a big sheet of paper — meerkats live in groups of 20 or more!

STEP 1

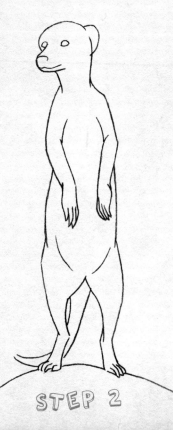

STEP 2

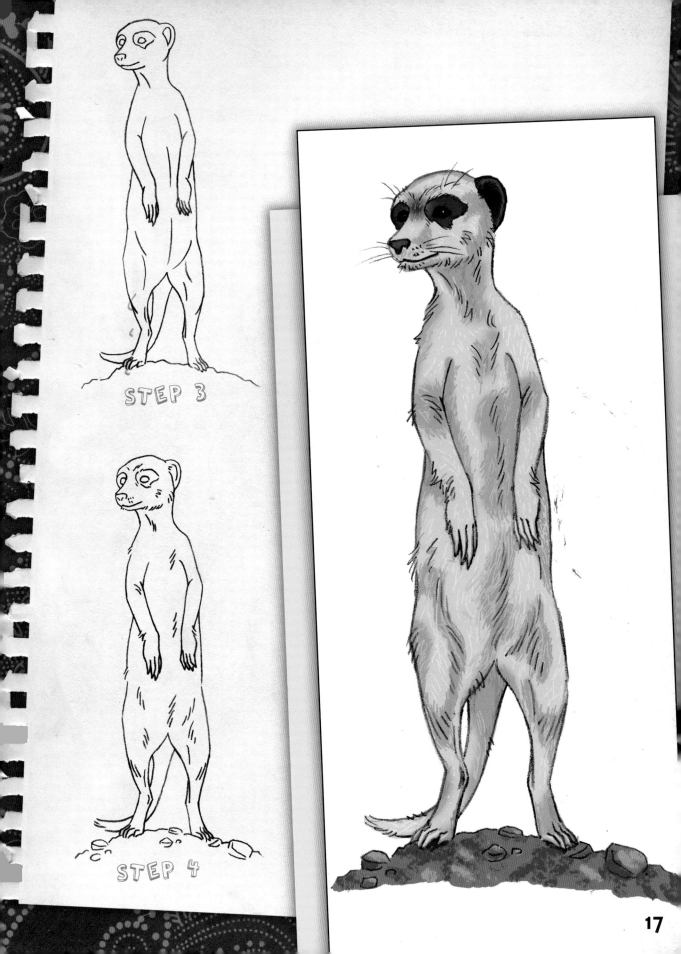

STEP 3

STEP 4

Panda

Pandas look like big black-and-white teddy bears. These gentle giants roam through China's bamboo forests in search of food. Each day, pandas spend more than 12 hours eating and finding food.

Once you've drawn one panda, draw another panda surrounded by a tall bamboo forest.

STEP 1

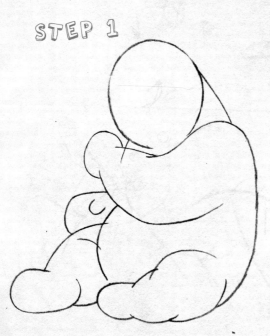

STEP 2

STEP 3

STEP 4

19

Puppy

Few things are cuter than a new puppy bouncing around on its big, clumsy paws. Most young dogs are filled with endless energy, and this one is no different. This playful puppy looks ready for a fun game of fetch.

Do you love short-legged basset hounds or wrinkly bulldogs? Try drawing your favorite dog breed.

STEP 1

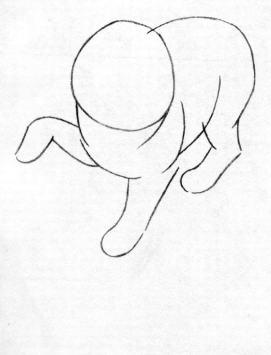

STEP 2

STEP 3

STEP 4

Sea Lion

They love to bark. They have whiskers and a long muzzle. You can even teach them to chase after balls. But they're not dogs — they're sea lions! Unlike dogs, these marine mammals wouldn't make good pets. That's because sea lions can weigh more than 600 pounds (272 kilograms).

Try drawing a group of sea lion pups lying on the beach.

STEP 1

STEP 2

STEP 3

STEP 4

Red-Eyed Tree Frog

Cute can come in all kinds of packages. Just ask the red-eyed tree frog. Sure, it's not fuzzy or cuddly. But this pint-sized amphibian wins you over with its neon green body and bright red peepers.

Try drawing a close-up of a frog's toes. Suction disks help the frog stick to leaves.

STEP 1

STEP 2

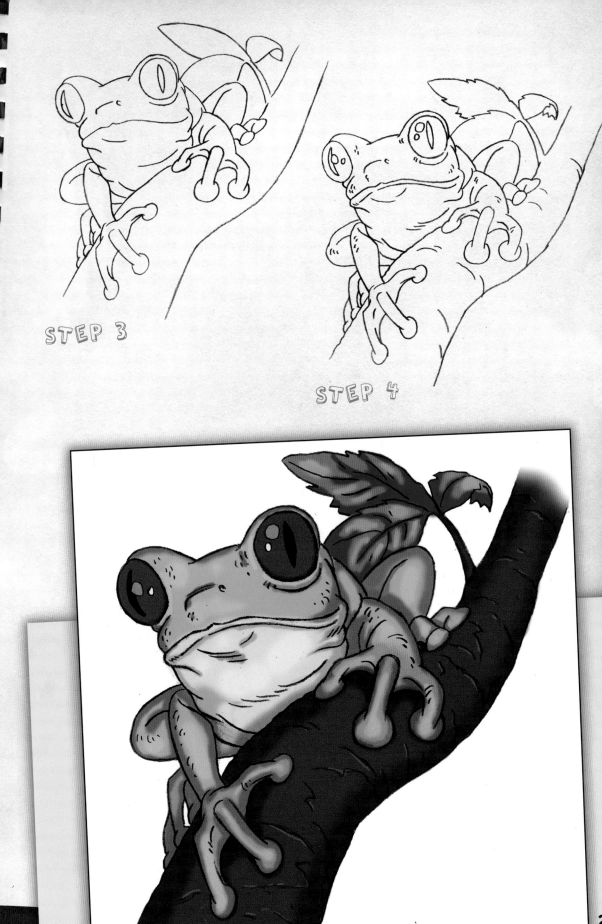

STEP 3

STEP 4

Penguin Family

Covered with black and white feathers, penguins look like they're wearing tiny tuxedos. The baby is still very young, so its feathers are soft and gray. But in a few months, it will look just like its parents.

Draw a parade of penguins marching across the ice.

STEP 1

STEP 2

STEP 3

STEP 4

To finish this drawing, turn to the next page. ⇨

STEP 5

STEP 6

Glossary

amphibian (am-FI-bee-uhn) — a cold-blooded animal with a backbone; amphibians live in water when young and can live on land as adults.

clan (KLAN) — a large group of animals living together

eucalyptus (yoo-kuh-LIP-tuhs) — a fragrant evergreen tree that grows in dry climates

feline (FEE-line) — any animal of the cat family

muzzle (MUHZ-uhl) — an animal's nose, mouth, and jaws

outback (OUT-bak) — a huge area in the middle of Australia that is covered by deserts and rocks

savanna (suh-VAN-uh) — a flat, grassy area of land with few or no trees

Read More

Clay, Kathryn. *How to Draw Horses*. Drawing Fun. Mankato, Minn.: Capstone Press, 2009.

Hart, Christopher. *Drawing Animals Made Amazingly Easy*. New York: Watson-Guptill Publications, 2007.

Walsh, Patricia. *Wild Animals*. Draw It! Chicago: Heinemann, 2006.

Internet Sites

FactHound offers a safe, fun way to find Internet sites related to this book. All of the sites on FactHound have been researched by our staff.

Here's all you do:

Visit *www.facthound.com*

FactHound will fetch the best sites for you!

Index